12 GREAT MOMENTS THAT CHANGED
INTERNET HISTORY

by Angie Smibert

www.12StoryLibrary.com

12-Story Library is an imprint of Peterson Publishing Company and Press Room Editions.

Produced for 12-Story Library by Red Line Editorial

Photographs ©: Reed Saxon/AP Images, cover, 1, 8; Fred Prouser/Corbis, 5; Elise Amendola/ AP Images, 6; Ricardo Alday/Shutterstock Images, 7; Jupiterimages/Thinkstock, 9; Lv jianshe/AP Images, 10, 29; Edgewater Media/Shutterstock Images, 11; Ben Margot/ AP Images, 12; Newscast/AP Image, 13; Lee Jin-Man/AP Images, 14; Elena Elisseeva/ Shutterstock Images, 16; Walter Bieri/AP Images, 17; Jan Haas/AP Images, 18; Uli Deck/ AP Images, 19; Jeff Chiu/AP Images, 20, 28; Cameron Bloch/AP Images, 22; Pablo Martinez Monsivais/AP Images, 24; Charles Dharapak/AP Images, 25; Thinkstock, 26; Mayra Beltran/ AP Images, 27

ISBN
978-1-63235-024-4 (hardcover)
978-1-63235-084-8 (paperback)
978-1-62143-065-0 (hosted ebook)

Library of Congress Control Number: 2014946803

Printed in the United States of America
Mankato, MN
October, 2014

Go beyond the book. Get free, up-to-date content on this topic at 12StoryLibrary.com.

TABLE OF CONTENTS

"LO" IS THE FIRST INTERNET MESSAGE

L.O. These two little letters were the start of something big. They changed the way people communicate, work, shop, play, learn, and even elect leaders. "LO" was the first message sent over the first computer network. That network would become the Internet.

It was a few days before Halloween in 1969. Charley Kline was a student at the University of California, Los Angeles (UCLA). He phoned a scientist at the Stanford Research

COMPUTERS IN 1969

Today, people carry powerful computers around in their book bags or pockets. In 1969, computers were enormous. Charley Kline's computer was approximately the size of a refrigerator. It weighed more than 900 pounds (408 kg). The host, or main, computer was much bigger. His computer acted like a bridge between the host computer and the one at Stanford.

74.8

Percentage of US homes with Internet access in 2012, up from 18 percent in 1997.

- A researcher at UCLA sent the first Internet message and a scientist at Stanford Research Institute received it.
- Their computers were hundreds of miles apart.
- These were the first two computers in a network called ARPANET.
- ARPANET would form the backbone of the Internet.

Institute hundreds of miles away. Both of them were sitting in front of computer terminals. Kline typed in a letter "L" on his keyboard. He asked the man on the phone, "Did you get the L?" He did. No one had sent a message over a computer network before. Kline was making history.

In the late 1960s, computers did not ask users to log in with a name and password. The computer waited for a command. Kline was typing a command: L-O-G-I-N. He pressed the "O" key. "Did you get the O?" he asked. The other man said yes.

Kline typed a "G." The computer on the other end crashed. Kline did not complete his command. Still, he and the Stanford scientist had done the important—and amazing—part. They had created the first computer network. It was called ARPANET.

Scientists working for the United States Defense Advanced Research Projects Agency (DARPA) invented ARPANET. By 1981, ARPANET connected more than 200 military and university computers. During the 1980s and 1990s, the network linked with other networks around the world, growing into the Internet we know today.

The room and equipment used to send the first Internet message

THE FIRST WEB PAGE GOES LIVE IN 1990

Nothing blinked, moved, or made a sound. There were no photos or videos. The page had a stark white background with a few words in black. A few in blue linked to other pages. The first web page was pretty plain. But it changed how we use the Internet.

Until 1990, people could share data, files, and messages on the Internet. However, nothing linked all of the information together. Tim Berners-Lee worked at CERN, a large

Tim Berners-Lee developed the World Wide Web.

Swiss research facility. Years earlier, he coded a program to keep track of all of the computers, files, and people at CERN. It helped him find information when he needed it. Berners-Lee wondered if he could do the same thing for the Internet.

Berners-Lee proposed the World Wide Web in 1989. He came up with the idea to give every document an address. He called that address a Uniform Resource Locator (URL). The URL tells other computers where to find the web page or document on the Internet. This allows pages to be linked together into a World Wide Web. Berners-Lee created the first web page on Christmas Day in 1990.

1 billion

Estimated number of web pages in July 2014.

- The first web page was very simple.
- Tim Berners-Lee designed the World Wide Web.
- The World Wide Web made it possible to connect information together.

Early web browsers changed the way people thought about the Internet.

http://www.theweb.com

MOSAIC

The World Wide Web was not very popular at first. People did not immediately realize the web was the ideal way to organize the Internet. It took a web browser called Mosaic to make them see the potential of the World Wide Web. A year after Mosaic was launched, web traffic increased 10,000-fold. Some people say that Mosaic made the Internet boom of the 1990s possible.

7

AMAZON REINVENTS ONLINE SHOPPING

Jeff Bezos founded Amazon in a garage in 1995.

On July 16, 1995, Amazon.com opened for business selling books online from a garage in Bellevue, Washington. A handful of people packed books on a table made out of an old door. In just a month, Amazon was selling to customers in all 50 states and 45 countries.

$2.29 billion

Amount spent shopping online on Cyber Monday in 2013.

- Amazon was founded in a garage.
- The employees packed books on an old door.
- At first, people were reluctant to shop online.
- Now the majority of Internet users make online purchases.

Amazon made it easy for people to shop for many items online.

In 1995, only a few businesses sold items online. At first, the idea of buying books or anything else online seemed strange to people. Customers were reluctant to give away personal information, such as credit card numbers, over the Internet. However, shoppers soon realized online shopping had its benefits. They could buy things online they could not find in their local stores. By 2000, 27 percent of Internet users had bought something online. In 2005, someone coined the term "Cyber Monday" to describe the online buying frenzy on the Monday after Thanksgiving. By 2010, more than two-thirds of all Internet users were online shoppers.

Today, Amazon's employees have grown from just a handful to more than 97,000. Employees work at Amazon facilities all over the world. The company had $74.45 billion in revenue in 2013. A year later, Jeff Bezos, Amazon's founder, was worth $29.9 billion.

WHO WANTS PIZZA?

The first thing bought online was not a book. It was a pizza. On September 9, 1994, someone ordered a pepperoni and mushroom pizza with extra cheese from Pizza Hut on its PizzaNet site.

EBAY MAKES ANYONE A SELLER—AND A BUYER

Over Labor Day weekend in 1995, Pierre Omidyar launched the website AuctionWeb. AuctionWeb was an experiment. Omidyar wanted to find out what would happen if every Internet user were able to buy and sell items online. The site allowed anyone to post an item for sale. Then, potential buyers would bid on the item until a set time period was up. The item went to the highest bidder.

The first item sold on AuctionWeb was a broken laser pointer. It sold for $14.98. Omidyar was surprised anyone had bought it. He e-mailed the bidder and asked if he knew the laser pointer was broken. The buyer replied that he collected broken laser pointers. This showed Omidyar that people have a

Millions of people across the world buy and sell items on eBay.

Omidyar was surprised people had an interest in broken laser pointers.

$140 million

Cost of the most expensive eBay item, a luxury yacht, in 2005.

- Pierre Omidyar wrote an auction website called AuctionWeb as an experiment.
- He sold a broken laser pointer and someone actually bought it.
- Omidyar changed the name to eBay.
- Millions use it every day to buy and sell.

passion for ordinary objects. He decided to build a business around it.

AuctionWeb soon outgrew Omidyar's original website. He changed the name to eBay in 1997. In a few years, 10 million people were using eBay to buy and sell goods online. In 2002, the company launched the "Buy It Now" feature. It allowed buyers to purchase items without bidding on them. By 2010, more items were purchased through the Buy It Now option than through auctions. In 2014, more than 120 million people actively used eBay.

GOOGLE BECOMES A VERB

In the early days of the World Wide Web, most search engines only looked for web pages with the most keywords. This did not always give the user the best results. Often, the results were not helpful.

In 1996, two Stanford University students,

Google founders Sergey Brin (left) and Larry Page

Sergey Brin and Larry Page, wanted to find a better way to search the web. They started a research project that would become Google. They were curious about how the world's web pages linked together. They analyzed the results from an early search engine called AltaVista.

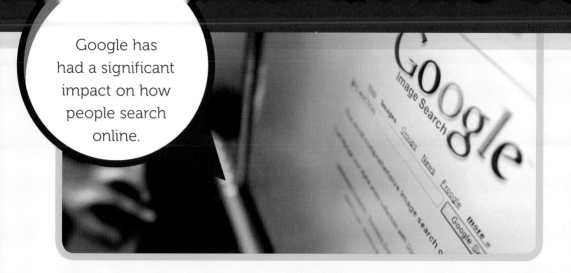

Google has had a significant impact on how people search online.

Its results listed the links between pages. Brin and Page noticed important pages had more links from other pages. If many people writing about cars linked one web page, that page must be more important than others. Brin and Page developed a system to rank web pages on their importance. They realized they could write a better search engine based on this page rank. Brin and Page founded Google in a friend's garage in 1998. By December of that year, *PC Magazine* called Google the top search engine of 1998.

Over the years, Google has expanded searching to include images, books, videos, and even places on Earth. In 2006, the Oxford English Dictionary added "to google" to the dictionary. The verb means to look for information on something

or someone using Google. In some dictionaries, "to google" means to simply search for something on the Internet.

1.2 trillion
Estimated number of Google searches users performed in 2012.

- Sergey Brin and Larry Page met at Stanford University.
- They figured out a way to search the web based on the importance of the page.
- Brin and Page founded Google in a friend's garage in 1998.
- "To google" has come to mean "to search the web."

A DANCING BABY GOES VIRAL

In the late 1990s, people saw it in their e-mail. They saw it on web sites. They saw it online. They sent it to friends. It was one of the very first viral videos.

A viral video is a form of an Internet meme. A meme is an idea that gets passed around from person to person. Internet memes can be videos, photos, text, or even just ideas. One of

Korean pop star Psy performing his viral hit "Gangnam Style."

2 billion

Number of views of the most viral video, "Gangnam Style," between its release and July 2014.

- The dancing baby was one of the first viral videos on the Internet.
- The video was so popular it even made it onto television.
- The dancing baby started as a sample file that came with 3-D animation software.

THINK ABOUT IT

There have been many other Internet memes since the dancing baby made its appearance. Ask an adult to help you research some others. Write a paragraph describing their popularity and significance.

the first internet memes was the phrase, "All Your Base Are Belong to Us." It came from a badly translated subtitle in a Japanese game called *Zero Wing*.

The first viral video was of a three-dimensional (3-D), animated baby dancing a cha-cha. The dancing baby was actually a sample file that came with the animation software Kinetix Character Studio. With the software, amateur animators could build 3-D characters with sophisticated

motions—such as dancing a cha-cha. The video became so popular that it was used in commercials, TV shows, games, and movies. The most famous use of the dancing baby was on the TV show *Ally McBeal* in 1998. This clip was set to the song, "Hooked on a Feeling." This particular version of the dancing baby went viral on the Internet again.

15

NAPSTER REVOLUTIONIZES THE MUSIC INDUSTRY

In June 1999, 19-year-old college students Sean Parker and Shawn Fanning wrote a computer program called Napster. They wanted to let friends connect and share music over the Internet. Before, people shared music by physically borrowing records, tapes, or CDs. Or they recorded a cassette tape or burned a CD and gave it to a friend.

WHAT IS COPYRIGHT?

An artist owns the exclusive legal right to his or her songs. This is called copyright. The artist gives the recording company the right to make a record and sell it. The artist and recording company split the profits. When people buy songs, they buy the right to play those songs for their own pleasure. However, they do not have the right to give or sell the songs to someone else.

Before Napster and Internet streaming, people shared music on CDs.

Napster let people make perfect digital copies of music on other users' computers. They could then download it to their own for free.

In a few months, the popularity of Napster had exploded beyond Parker and Fanning's college campus. The music industry sued Napster. Recording companies and artists argued Napster allowed people to steal their music. In 2001, a court agreed. Napster had to stop letting people share copyrighted music.

It also had to pay millions in fines. This put the original Napster out of business.

However, Napster made the idea of sharing music digitally popular. Record companies soon learned that releasing free digital music actually increased sales of CDs. Though gone now, Napster paved the way for legal file sharing and music sites such as iTunes, Spotify, Rhapsody, and Pandora.

iTunes is a legal way to download and share music.

17

WIKIPEDIA HELPS PEOPLE SHARE KNOWLEDGE

Wikipedia founder Jimmy Wales wanted to put all the knowledge in the world at people's fingertips for free. On January 16, 2001, he typed the words "Hello World" on the first Wikipedia page. The next day, he asked for volunteers to help write and edit a new kind of online encyclopedia.

In a month, Wikipedia had 1,000 articles.

The technology behind Wikipedia was not new. The technology is called "wiki." Creator Ward Cunningham chose the name wiki because it means "quick" in Hawaiian. Wiki is an application that allows people to work together to quickly write and edit website content. Anybody can write and edit any entry in Wikipedia. Thousands of volunteers from all over the world work together. They make sure everything is written according to

Wikipedia founder Jimmy Wales at a conference in Germany in 2014

2,002

Number of volumes the English version of Wikipedia would fill if printed like the *Encyclopedia Britannica*.

- Jimmy Wales founded Wikipedia to give everyone free access to knowledge.
- The first entry said, "Hello World."
- Wikipedia uses volunteers to write and edit articles.

THINK ABOUT IT

Wikipedia has made it very easy to learn about many different topics. But not all articles are written by experts. How can you know that the information you read there is accurate? Make a list of the pros and cons of having an online encyclopedia written and edited by anyone.

Wikipedia's rules. Thirteen years after Wales typed "Hello World," Wikipedia had 4.5 million articles in English alone. In July 2014, Wikipedia had 32.9 million articles in 285 languages.

German is one of 285 languages in which Wikipedia articles are written.

NUPEDIA

Wikipedia started as a companion to an online encyclopedia called Nupedia. Nupedia was professionally written and edited. However, Wikipedia proved far more popular. Nupedia folded in 2003.

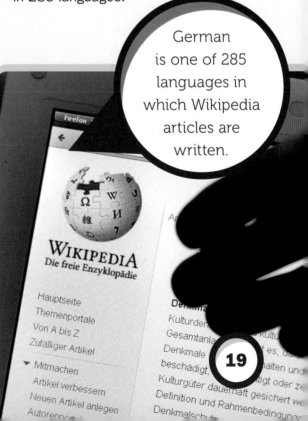

FACEBOOK PIONEERS SOCIAL MEDIA

The social media site Facebook changed the way people connect and share with others across the world. In 2004, Mark Zuckerberg founded "the Facebook" in his Harvard University dorm room. He wanted to help Harvard students and alumni connect with each other. Within 24 hours, 1,200 Harvard students had signed up. A month and a half later, 50 percent of Harvard students had a Facebook profile.

Zuckerberg realized Facebook could be popular with students

Mark Zuckerberg announces a new look for Facebook's News Feed in 2013.

$31 billion

Net worth of Facebook founder Mark Zuckerberg.

- Mark Zuckerberg started Facebook in his dorm room.
- Facebook was first only for Harvard students and alumni.
- There were more than 1 billion Facebook users in 2014.

at other schools, too. By 2005, Facebook had reached college campuses around the world. A year later, Facebook became available to anyone. People no longer had to be college students to join. On July 21, 2010, Zuckerberg announced that Facebook had 500 million active users. If it were a country, it would rank right behind China and India in population. Facebook was the first social media site to reach that many people.

SOCIAL MEDIA IN THE NEWS

Social media sites have changed the way people report and read the news. Many people share news reports they read or view online through Facebook and Twitter. Newspapers, news radio stations, and news TV stations use their websites to share the news. Many also have social media accounts to reach more readers and viewers. They often use these sites to share and follow breaking news stories.

By 2014, more than 1 billion people were on Facebook. Today, people use Facebook to maintain friendships over long distances. Businesses use it to connect with customers. Facebook has changed how people interact.

YOUTUBE MAKES SHARING VIDEOS EASY

On April 23, 2005, three friends posted an 18-second video on the website YouTube. The video showed one of them standing in front of an elephant cage at a zoo. This was the first YouTube video.

In 2004, the friends worked together at PayPal, an Internet payment

> YouTube made it easy for people to upload and share videos.

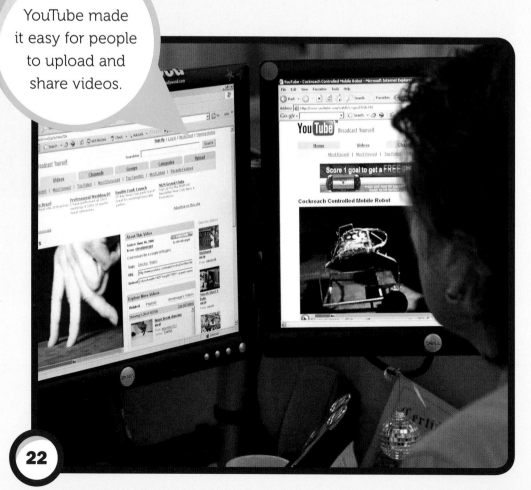

18

Length, in seconds, of the first YouTube video.

- Three friends founded YouTube to make video sharing easy.
- The first video they posted was about a trip to the zoo.
- Google bought YouTube in 2006.

company. They noticed viral videos were spreading faster and faster on the Internet. For instance, 2.3 million people watched a video of comedian Jon Stewart's appearance on CNN. That was three times as many people who actually saw it on television. In 2004, a tsunami hit the countries around the Indian Ocean. Many people recorded the wave and its destruction using their cell phones. Those videos circulated around the world.

However, uploading and sharing the videos was not technically easy. In 2005, the three friends founded the website YouTube. YouTube made it easy to upload and share videos.

WATCHING AND LEARNING

Funny cats, dancing babies, and other viral videos are not the only things to watch on YouTube. Many people use YouTube to learn. Videos cover all sorts of topics. Experts in science, math, history, and literature all produce YouTube videos. Some videos show the teacher talking to a group. Others use animated videos and other images to help teach. Many schools and universities have their own YouTube accounts.

Just a few months later, YouTube celebrated its first video with a million views. YouTube proved so popular that Google bought it in 2006 for $1.65 billion.

THE INTERNET HELPS ELECT A PRESIDENT

The 2008 US presidential election was historic for many reasons. Barack Obama was the first racial minority candidate elected president in the United States. It was also the year when the Internet played a major role in who won. Some historians have even said President Obama may not have won the election without the Internet.

Facebook and other social media played a large role in the 2008 election.

During the 2008 presidential election, 55 percent of Americans went online to learn more about the candidates. They also used it to get involved in the political process. They followed election news and shared their views with others on social media sites. Citizens also used fact-checking sites on the Internet to find out if what candidates said was true.

Obama continued to use YouTube after he was elected.

The 2008 election was also the first time all candidates tried to connect with voters through social media. Candidates used the Internet to reach voters, raise money, and even organize their campaigns. Barack Obama was the most successful candidate at using the Internet to reach the public. His campaign used social media to reach younger voters. His social media team even included one of the founders of Facebook. Obama's team used the web to raise money and organize supporters. His campaign used YouTube to deliver speeches and responses.

52.93

Percentage of the popular vote Barack Obama received in 2008.

- Most voters went online to find out about candidates.
- All candidates used websites and social media to reach voters, raise money, and organize their campaigns.
- President Obama's team used it most effectively.

12

MILLIONS ORGANIZE ON SOCIAL MEDIA

On January 25, 2011, millions of protestors across Egypt demanded the overthrow of President Hosni Mubarak. Unlike a US president, Mubarak was not elected and had ruled Egypt for 30 years. He resigned 18 days later. Ordinary people organized these protests using Facebook and Twitter. Young Egyptians used the hashtags #Egypt

Cairo, Egypt, was only one North African city to experience protests in the Arab Spring.

230,000

Number of daily Egyptian tweets about the political change in Egypt at the peak of the uprising there.

- Egyptians used social media to organize protests in January 2011.
- They used the hashtags #Jan25 and #Egypt.
- The Egyptian government shut down the Internet.
- Egypt was just one country in a wave of political protests during Arab Spring.

and #Jan25 on Twitter to spread the word about the revolution. The government responded by shutting down the Internet. Mubarak stepped down a few days later.

The Egyptian people were not the only ones to use social media to organize protests. During late

THINK ABOUT IT

Social media helped people in the Middle East organize protests. How could it help you make changes at your school? List at least three ways you could use social media to make positive changes.

2010 and early 2011, people in other Middle Eastern countries did the same. These protests became known as the Arab Spring. A wave of demonstrations, protests, and riots swept through the Middle East. They started in the North African country of Tunisia and spread across the region. People were frustrated with the rule of dictators and corruption. They protested human rights violations and the poverty in their countries. They used social media to organize these actions.

Egyptian protesters used social media and the Internet to coordinate and spread news.

27

FACT SHEET

- The Internet began in response to Sputnik. The Soviet Union launched the world's first satellite in 1957. Fearing the Russians would beat America in the race to build new technologies, the US government started DARPA. One of DARPA's projects was a global computer network called ARPANET. During the 1970s and 1980s, most people did not know this network existed. ARPANET was restricted to the military and universities doing defense research.

- In 1990, three events happened that opened up the Internet to everyone. ARPANET was shut down. Commercial activity was allowed on the Internet. And the World Wide Web linked together information like never before.

- The 1990s became the decade of the Internet boom. Many businesses made a great deal of money selling goods and services online. Others were not as successful. eBay enabled the average person to sell and buy directly with someone across the globe.

- In the early twenty-first century, more and more people gained access to faster and faster Internet. The Internet changed how people listen to music, watch videos, take classes, share their lives, and even participate in politics.

GLOSSARY

copyrighted
Written, musical, or artistic work that someone has the exclusive right to make copies of.

hashtag
A word or phrase used within a social media message to identify a topic.

Internet
A vast computer network linking smaller computer networks worldwide.

keywords
Words of interest or significance.

meme
An image, video, or idea that is copied and spread rapidly by Internet users.

search engines
Websites that search other websites for keywords.

social media
Websites where users can create and share information.

Uniform Resource Locator
An address—such as www.whitehouse.gov—that identifies a particular website or page on the Internet.

viral
Becoming very popular by being shared quickly online.

web browser
A computer program people use to access the Internet.

FOR MORE INFORMATION

Books

Gilbert, Sarah. *Built for Success: The Story of Amazon.com*. Mankato, MN: Creative Paperbacks. 2013. Print.

McPherson, Stephanie Sammartino. *Tim Berners-Lee: Inventor of the World Wide Web*. Minneapolis, MN: Twenty-First Century Books, 2010. Print.

Yomtov, Nel. *Internet Inventors*. New York: Children's Press, 2013. Print.

Websites

The Birth of the Web
www.home.web.cern.ch/topics/birth-web

Invention of the Internet
www.history.com/topics/inventions/invention-of-the-internet

Nerds 2.0.1
www.pbs.org/opb/nerds2.0.1/index.html

INDEX

About the Author

Angie Smibert is the author of several young adult science fiction novels, numerous short stories, and a few educational titles. She also worked at NASA's Kennedy Space Center for many, many years. She received NASA's prestigious Silver Snoopy as well as several other awards.

Lakeview Public Library
1120 Woodfield Road
Rockville Centre, New York 11570
(516) 536-3071
lakeview@nassaulibrary.org

28,50